EXPLORERS

OF THE

DEEPEST

PLACES

ON EARTH

by Peter Mavrikis

raintree

a Capstone company — publishers for children

Raintree is an imprint of Capstone Global Library Limited, a company incorporated in England and Wales having its registered office at 264 Banbury Road, Oxford, OX2 7DY – Registered company number: 6695582

www.raintree.co.uk
myorders@raintree.co.uk

Edited by Anna Butzer
Designed by Kayla Rossow
Original illustrations © Capstone Global Library Limited 2021
Picture research by Tracy Cummins
Production by Katy LaVigne
Originated by Capstone Global Library Ltd
Printed and bound in India

978 1 3982 0354 9 (hardback)
978 1 3982 0353 2 (paperback)

British Library Cataloguing in Publication Data
A full catalogue record for this book is available from the British Library.

Acknowledgements
We would like to thank the following for permission to reproduce photographs: Alamy: Alain Le Garsmeur Dr Sylvia Earle, 14, Album, 25, Everett Collection Inc, 8; Getty Images: Bettmann, 7, 13, Jason LaVeris/FilmMagic, 22, SAEED KHAN/AFP, 21; National Geographic Image Collection: STEPHEN ALVAREZ, 17; Science Source: Connie Bransilver, 15; Shutterstock: Paul Vinten, 5, Sementer, 19, Sergey Novikov, Cover, 1; Strand Photography: Hans Strand, 26, 28, 29; Wikimedia: NOAA Ship Collection, 11

Every effort has been made to contact copyright holders of material reproduced in this book. Any omissions will be rectified in subsequent printings if notice is given to the publisher.

CONTENTS

Words in **bold** are in the glossary.

DEEP, DARK UNKNOWN

Earth is full of mystery and wonder. There's a lot we do not know about the deepest parts of Earth. New information is hidden far below the surface of the oceans or at the bottom of dark caves.

Our planet's hidden and unreachable depths have captured the imagination of people going back thousands of years. To help explain the unknown and unexplored, early humans told stories. These stories became the myths and legends that many of us know today. Some stories are about giant sea creatures that live deep in the ocean. Others are about lost underwater cities.

Scientists and explorers have been working to uncover secrets in Earth's deepest places. Some are going where humans have never been. As they explore, they are discovering new species of plants and animals, and learning more about the deep workings of our planet.

Some explorers travel deep into underwater caves hoping to make discoveries.

Chapter 1

JACQUES PICCARD AND DONALD WALSH

On 23 January 1960, Jacques Piccard and Donald Walsh travelled down to the Mariana Trench in the Pacific Ocean. The goal of the mission was simple: to see if it was possible to reach the deepest part of the world's oceans.

Full submersion

Their vessel, the *Trieste*, was unlike any other seacraft. It was a bathyscaphe. The craft measured 15 metres (50 feet) in length. It was made up of two sections: a large float chamber and a smaller **pressure** sphere. The float chamber was filled with petrol air tanks to create **buoyancy**. It was the part of the craft that would help the explorers rise back to the surface. The pressure sphere was barely large enough to fit the two explorers. It was located beneath the chamber.

The *Trieste*'s crew cabin below the chamber was made of heavy steel. This material helped it withstand pressure in deep water.

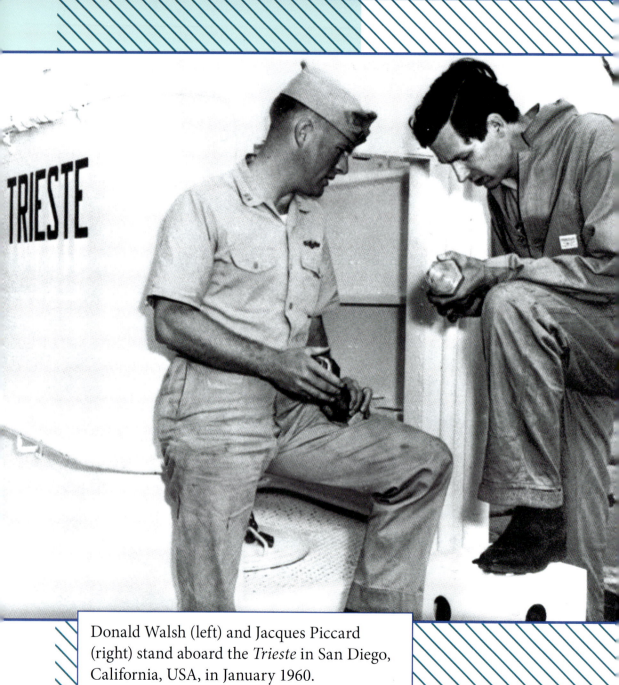

Donald Walsh (left) and Jacques Piccard (right) stand aboard the *Trieste* in San Diego, California, USA, in January 1960.

Under pressure

With rough seas and strong winds, the two explorers entered the cramped pressure sphere and began their descent into the dark depths of the Pacific Ocean. The ride was not easy. At a depth of about 9,144 m (30,000 feet), they heard a thunderous *crack!* The immense pressure of the deep was squeezing the craft and caused the viewing window to crack. Piccard and Walsh checked that all systems were working, and the mission moved forward. After travelling in the dark waters for almost 5 hours, the *Trieste* reached the ocean floor. They were 10,916 m (35,813 feet) below the surface. They were deeper than any human had ever reached!

Signs of life

Once they reached the ocean floor, the men were surprised to find life. They discovered small, strange-looking fish. They also saw a type of flatfish and shrimp. These amazing discoveries proved to scientists that life could exist at this depth.

Concerned about the loud crack they had heard on the way down, Piccard and Walsh began their return to the surface after 20 minutes. The journey back to the waiting support ship took 3 hours and 15 minutes. Luckily for the two men, the damaged window did not break.

FACT

Sunlight from the ocean surface cannot be seen beyond 1,005 m (3,300 feet). At this depth, the ocean is pitch black. It is called the Midnight Zone.

From inside the small crew cabin, Piccard and Walsh made discoveries about deep-sea life.

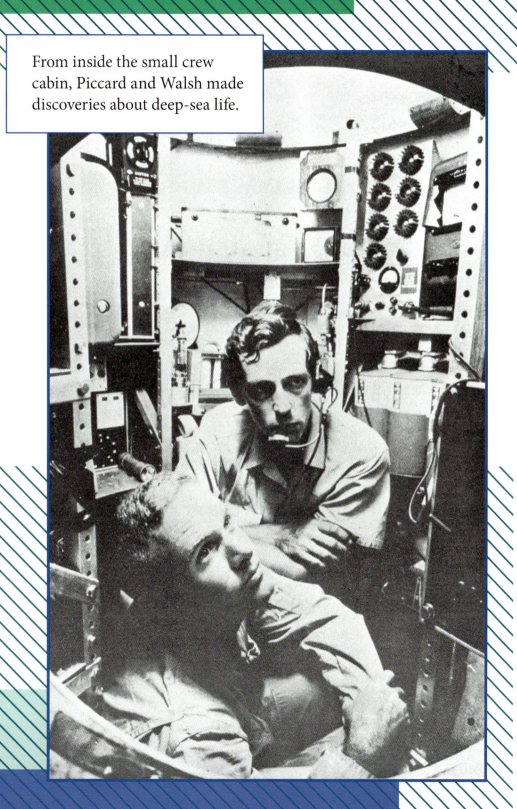

Chapter 2

SYLVIA EARLE

Sylvia Earle is an American marine **biologist**, explorer, writer and **conservationist**. The world's oceans caught Earle's imagination at a very young age. This early interest in the sea inspired her to explore the mysteries of the deep. It also earned her the nickname "Her Deepness".

Solo diver

In 1979, off the coast of the island of Oahu, Hawaii, Earle set the world record for the deepest **solo** dive. Protected by a bulky metal suit, she **descended** 381 m (1,250 feet). Once she reached the bottom, Earle walked on the ocean floor for 2.5 hours.

Earle's dive was **untethered**. She was not attached to a surface ship. This would have made a rescue difficult if she'd had a problem and needed to resurface. But working untethered had its benefits. It allowed Earle to walk freely on the seabed and witness life on the bottom of the ocean. One animal that Earle saw firsthand was the bamboo coral. This sea creature can grow up to 2 m (6 feet) in length. It gives off a blue light when touched.

The metal suit that Earle (right) wore on her record-breaking dive is called a JIM suit.

Setting another record

In 1985, Earle set another record. This time, she was joined by her husband, Graham Hawkes. He is a submarine designer and marine engineer. Together, they built the **submersible** *Deep Rover*. In this sub, they were able to reach a depth of 1,000 m (3,300 feet). Unlike the awkward metal suit, the *Deep Rover* was easy to move around in the water.

Sylvia Earle and Graham Hawkes worked together on marine projects.

Earle holds a crab while scuba diving near the Florida Keys.

>>> Protecting the seas

Earle has witnessed the wonders of the sea, but has also seen the damage to oceans caused by pollution and overfishing. For the last 20 years, Earle has dedicated her life to protecting the world's oceans. She is the founder of Mission Blue, an organization that creates protected areas for marine life around the world.

Chapter 3

GENNADY VIKTOROVICH SAMOKHIN

Krubera Cave is the second-deepest known cave in the world. It reaches a depth of 2,197 m (7,208 feet). Located in the country of Georgia in Eastern Europe, it was first discovered in the early 1960s. In early attempts to explore the cave, explorers were only able to go down about 300 m (1,000 feet). It was not until 2012 when Ukrainian diver and **speleologist** Gennady Viktorovich Samokhin broke the cave diving record. He travelled down to a depth of 2,196 m (7,205 feet).

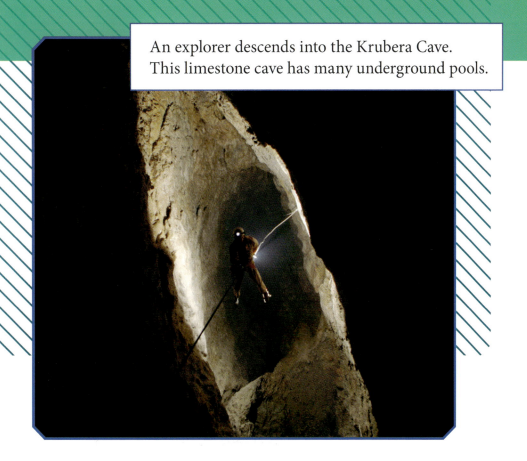

An explorer descends into the Krubera Cave. This limestone cave has many underground pools.

Risks and dangers

Samokhin's **expedition** stretched over five weeks and included a team of 59 researchers and scientists. Like many journeys to unknown parts of the world, there is always risk and danger. For cave divers, concerns include getting stuck in tight spaces, flooding and, as always, the risk of injury from a fall. Physical and mental preparation is very important before any exploration even begins.

The right equipment

For Samokhin, the 2012 expedition made him the first person to travel down to the deepest-known part of the cave. Getting there was not easy. The equipment Samokhin needed for the expedition included climbing ropes and harnesses, as well as air tanks and other diving equipment. The expedition also called for gas stoves, 3,000 batteries and 500 kilograms (1,100 pounds) of food!

In addition to surveying and mapping out the cave, the team members found new species of animals. In the deepest part of the cave, scientists found tiny, eyeless insects called springtails and a new species of transparent fish.

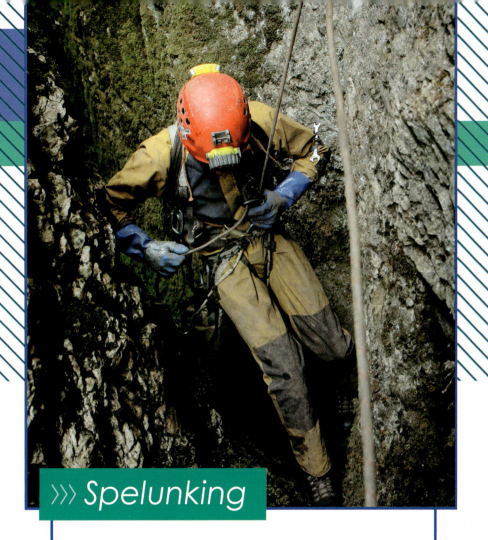

>>> Spelunking

The activity of exploring caves is called caving or spelunking. Hobbyist and extreme explorers who enjoy the challenge of spelunking are called cavers. Like other outdoor activities, including hiking, mountain climbing and skiing, spelunking requires special types of equipment. This includes protective hard hats, torches, knee pads and strong ropes for travelling down and going back up vertical cave openings. Tens of thousands of people around the world are members of spelunking clubs.

Chapter **4**

JAMES CAMERON

James Cameron is a Canadian filmmaker, deep-sea explorer and **environmentalist**. He has worked on many Hollywood blockbusters, including *The Abyss* and *Titanic*, which helped develop his interest in deep-sea exploration. On 26 March 2012, Cameron piloted the *Deepsea Challenger* to the deepest-known part of the planet: Challenger Deep.

Cameron sat inside a scale model of the *Deepsea Challenger*'s pilot chamber at the Australian National Maritime Museum in 2018.

The *Deepsea Challenger* was on display at the California Science Center in 2013. The seacraft was designed to float down vertically in the water so Cameron could travel down quickly.

Challenger Deep

Located in the Pacific Ocean, the Challenger Deep is part of the Mariana Trench. The lowest part of the Challenger Deep lies between 10,898 and 10,928 m (35,755 and 35,855 feet) below sea level. Fifty years earlier, Jacques Piccard and Donald Walsh made a similar journey in the *Trieste*. Cameron, however, set a record by making the deep-sea dive alone and reaching a depth of 10,908 m (35,787 feet).

Danger, danger everywhere

James Cameron was well aware of the risks involved in the dive. No matter how much he trained or prepared, danger was everywhere. Concerns included vessel malfunction, communication failure, freezing, fire and getting crushed by the immense pressure. Luckily, he did not encounter any of these problems.

Filming the dive

It took Cameron 2 hours and 36 minutes to reach the ocean floor. As a film director, he made sure he filmed the entire trip. This helped provide scientists and researchers with valuable information. The *Deepsea Challenger* was also equipped with a robotic arm. This allowed Cameron to collect samples. The deep-sea submersible also had equipment that measured temperature, pressure and other conditions on the ocean floor.

The trip back to the surface took 70 minutes. James Cameron became the third person to reach the Mariana Trench. And for a time, he was the only one to have made the journey alone.

A boom stuck out from the *Deepsea Challenger*'s side to hold a camera and other equipment.

FACT

Scientists weren't the only ones that got to see Cameron's historic voyage. In 2014, the filmmaker and explorer released a film, *Deepsea Challenge 3D*. It allowed cinema-goers to see what his record-setting journey to the ocean floor was like.

Chapter 5

FREYSTEINN SIGMUNDSSON

Dr Freysteinn Sigmundsson is an Icelandic scientist and volcano researcher. In October 2010, he became the first person to walk inside a **magma** chamber of a volcano.

Once inside Thrihnukagigur, Sigmundsson was able to see what the walls looked like.

A sleeping giant

Thrihnukagigur, which means "Three Peaks Crater" in Icelandic, covers an area of 3,270 square metres (35,198 square feet) and is 213 m (699 feet) deep. Discovered in 1974, Thrihnukagigur is a **dormant** volcano. It last erupted over 3,000 years ago. A dormant volcano is like a sleeping giant. It can wake up and erupt at any moment!

Inside a volcano

The expedition set off from Iceland's capital, Reykjavik. It consisted of 17 scientists and support staff, including mountain climbers. Using climbing equipment, the explorers descended down the crater of the volcano. Once inside, the team explored the three magma chambers.

A look inside

Exploring the magma chambers gave Sigmundsson and his team a firsthand view of how volcanoes work. Looking at the "plumbing" allowed the scientists to better understand the movement of magma from inside the volcano. The information collected from Sigmundsson and his team will help researchers better understand volcanoes.

Sigmundsson and another expedition team member examined rock inside Thrihnukagigur.

››› *Liquid rock*

Magma chambers are where volcanoes store the molten (liquid) rock that rises from deep below Earth's surface. When a volcano erupts, magma and other gases are released into the air. Built-up pressure from deep inside the volcano pushes the magma out. Volcanic eruptions are very dangerous and can cause a lot of damage. Deadly gases, smoke and rocks blow high into the air. Molten rock also pours out and spreads across the land until it cools and hardens.

Glossary

biologist scientist who studies living things

buoyancy ability to float on water

conservationist someone who works to protect Earth's natural resources

descend travel downwards

dormant not active; dormant volcanoes have not erupted for many years

environmentalist person who is concerned about nature and works to help protect it

expedition journey taken by a group of people for a specific reason, including exploration

magma melted rock found under Earth's surface

pressure force produced by pressing on something

solo alone

speleologist person who explores caves

submersible sea vessel that operates underwater

untethered not connected to another object

Find out more

Books

Deep Oceans (Earth's Last Frontiers), Ellen Labrecque (Raintree, 2015)

Explorers: Amazing Tales of the World's Greatest Adventures, Nellie Huang (DK Children, 2019)

Volcanologist (Coolest Jobs on the Planet), Hugh Tuffen with Melanie Waldron (Raintree, 2015)

Websites

www.bbc.co.uk/news/science-environment-17013285
Dive down to the deepest depths of the ocean!

www.dkfindout.com/uk/earth/caves
Find out more about caves.

Index